help**me**
BECOME™

Becoming **Honest** &
Overcoming **Lying**™

REAL
**mvp**kids™

# Lock Up Lying™

## SOPHIA DAY®

Written by Kayla Pearson    Illustrated by Timothy Zowada

# WELCOME to the WORLD OF

## mvpkids®

Entertainment with **PURPOSE**™

Everything we create is with the intention of nurturing a child's character. Our mission is to equip parents, teachers, and caregivers to engage with kids through inspiring entertainment.

nurture
**LITERACY**™

cultivate
**MENTORSHIP**™

inspire
**CHARACTER**®

expand
**EDUCATION**™

enrich
**ENTERTAINMENT**™

help me
BECOME™

Becoming *Honest* &
Overcoming **Lying**™

REAL
**mvp**kids®

# Lock Up Lying™

## SOPHIA DAY®

Written *by* Kayla Pearson    Illustrated *by* Timothy Zowada

**The Sophia Day® Creative Team-**
Kayla Pearson, Timothy Zowada,
Megan Johnson, Stephanie Strouse, Mel Sauder

A **special thank you** to our team of reviewers who graciously
give us feedback, edits, and help ensure that our products
remain accurate, applicable, and genuinely diverse.

Published and Distributed by MVP Kids Media, LLC -
Mesa, Arizona, USA
Printed by Prosperous Printing Inc. - Shenzhen, China
Designed by Stephanie Strouse

DOM Jan 2020, Job #13-003-01

*May your childhood be filled with adventure, your days with hope, and your learnings with wisdom, and may you continuously grow as an MVP Kid, preparing to lead a responsible, meaningful life.*

-SOPHIA DAY

# TABLE OF CONTENTS

# Liam Learns to be a Doctor

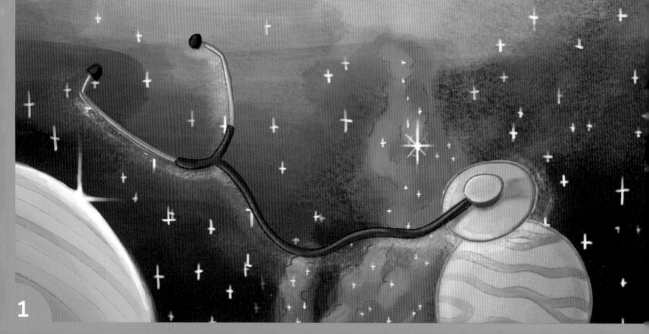

Buh-Bump!
Buh-Bump!

Liam was excited to hear a heartbeat as he used a stethoscope.

This year, Liam was finally old enough to go to La Paz City Children's Hospital with his mom, Dr. Johnson, for *Bring Your Child to Work Day*.

Everything they did was so much **better** than Liam expected.

Liam got to see and touch **real** organs.

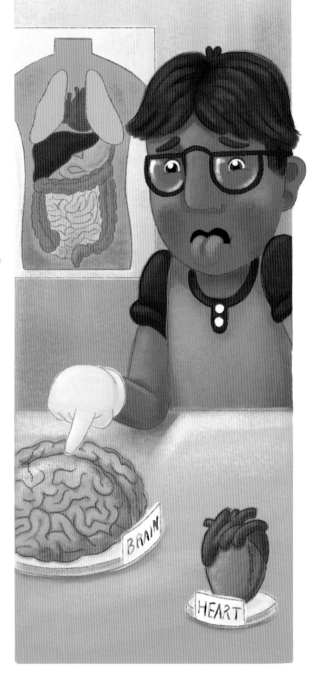

He learned where to feel for a pulse on his wrist.

They even performed a mock surgery in an operating room!

Next, the group went to the MRI room. The leader explained how important technology is to doctors.

"Machines like this one help doctors understand what is going on inside your body— things they can't see from the outside." They each took turns lying on the MRI table.

As Liam was waiting his turn, he noticed some buttons on the machine. Curious about what would happen, Liam pressed the button.

Beep!
Beep!
Beep!

The table began to slowly slide into the machine.

8

The leader came over
right away and pushed
the button again. The
table stopped. She looked
at Liam and the kids
standing there.

"I'm going to ask which one of you pressed the button, and I need you to **choose to tell the truth.**"

# Liam *didn't* want to tell the truth.

He didn't want to get in trouble.

What if she made him leave the group and go home?

But what would happen if he lied?

Liam looked at the other kids. If he said he didn't do it, would they all get in trouble?

Liam didn't want anyone else to get in trouble for something he did. Liam decided to tell the truth. "It was me. I pressed the button."

"Thank you for **telling the truth,** Liam. Pressing buttons could get someone hurt. You'll need to stay close to me and be my helper for the rest of the day. I'll help you keep your hands safe."

Slowly, Liam walked to the front of the line with the leader. Even though he was a little embarrassed, he was glad he didn't lie and get the other kids in trouble.

The rest of the day, Liam learned a lot about doctors and how **telling the truth** to doctors is so important.

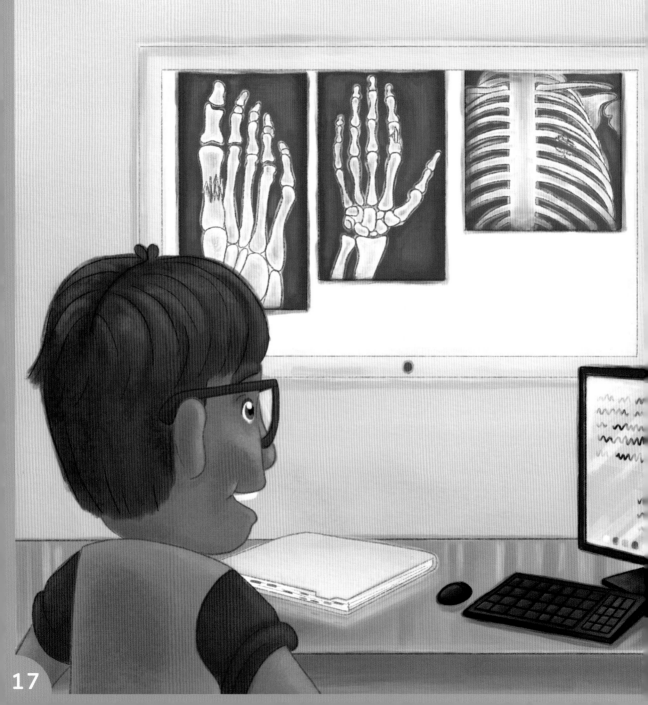

When the day was finished, he told his mom about everything he learned...and he told the **whole truth** about what happened. His mom was proud he chose to be honest.

# THINK & TALK ABOUT IT

*Discuss the story...*

1.  Why was Liam at the hospital?

2.  What kinds of things did Liam learn?

3.  Why did Liam press the button?

4.  What might have happened if Liam lied?

5.  How did Liam feel when he told the truth?

*For additional tips and reference information, visit **www.mvpkids.com**.*

*Discuss how to apply the story...*

1. What does it mean to tell the truth?

2. Why do you think it is important to tell the truth?

3. Describe a time you chose to tell either a truth or a lie. Which did you choose? Why?

4. What happens when you choose to lie?

5. Even if it means you might get in trouble, will you choose to tell the truth?

*FOR PARENTS & MENTORS: Knowing how to respond to a child who has lied depends on their developmental stage. Children choose to lie for different reasons at different ages. Toddlers might tell lies to get something they want, but may not understand the concept of lying. When children are in preschool they may begin making up stories as a way of processing new ideas. As children enter into elementary school, they are able to understand the difference between telling the truth, a lie, and storytelling. At this age, they might tell more lies to see what they can get away with.*

*Children often lie to avoid punishment. Asking questions when you already know the answer may corner a child into telling a lie. Instead, present the question in a way that encourages children to choose to tell the truth. When children choose honesty, be sure to praise them for it.*

# Julia's BIG Shot

Julia sat on the sideline of the soccer field. Her dad coached a team and would bring Julia and her little brother, Victor, to watch.

Toward the end of practice, Julia and Victor would come onto the field to play with the team.

At the penalty line, Julia kicked the soccer ball hard, but it went over the goal.

"Nice try, Julia!
Next time lean over the ball more.
Victor gets a shot now!" said Papá.

# "Victor! Victor! Victor!"

Victor **always** seemed to get more attention from the team.

This made Julia feel *jealous*.
*Urrgg. I wish I would have made that goal*, thought Julia.

Victor shot the ball low and to the corner.

# Victor scored!

The team ran up and gave Victor high fives.

"Practice is over! Good job tonight, team!"
Everyone ran to the sideline to grab some water.

"Way to go, little man!"

"We could use your awesome skills on our team."

"Are you sure you're only five?"

Julia did not like that Victor was getting all the attention, so she blurted out, "I scored three goals at my game last Saturday! And I can juggle the ball fifty times without it dropping!"

She had only scored one goal and she wasn't very good at juggling. She just wanted to impress them. She wanted them to see she was a great soccer player, too.

"Fifty times?! Wow, that's pretty impressive. Let's see you do it," one of the players challenged her. Julia tried to get out of it, but the players insisted she show them.

"One, two, three, four..."

The team counted out loud with each bounce.
She tried a couple of times but never made it
past ten. She kept trying, but the players slowly
began to leave.

Finally, Papá came over to speak with Julia. "Julia, why did you tell the team you could do something when you are not able to do that yet?"

"You are a great soccer player. Everyone misses a shot sometimes, but that does not make you a bad player. You shouldn't lie to make yourself look better than others."

"I wish I would have never said that.
Now, I look even worse."

"You should have congratulated your brother and been honest about your skills. That would have impressed the team. Remember, you don't have to prove yourself to others, but practice to improve yourself for you."

Julia hugged her dad and helped carry the cones back to the car. From now on she was going to be honest about her skills and work hard to be the best she could be.

# THINK & TALK
# ABOUT IT

## Julia's Big Shot

*Discuss the story...*

1. What was Julia doing at the soccer field?

2. What happened that made Julia feel jealous?

3. Why did Julia choose to lie?

4. How did lying make things worse?

5. What should Julia have done differently?

*For additional tips and reference information, visit* **www.mvpkids.com**.

39

*Discuss how to apply the story...*

1. Do you think the other players will trust what Julia says next time?

2. Was there a time when you lied and someone found out? How did lying make things worse?

3. Julia felt embarrassed when she missed the goal. Tell about a time when you felt embarrassed.

4. Julia felt jealous when her brother was getting more attention from the team. Tell about a time when you felt jealous.

5. What is something other than lying that you can do when you feel embarrassed or jealous?

**FOR PARENTS & MENTORS:** *Any healthy relationship, whether between family members or friends, is based on trust. Without honesty, trust is not possible. This is one reason why teaching a child to tell the truth is so important. Talk with your child about how lying doesn't help situations. Oftentimes, lying has natural consequences, such as the loss of trust or the embarrassment of getting caught (like what happened in the story with Julia). When this happens, be sure to talk with your child about how being honest is always a better choice. Admit that telling the truth may take courage, but help them recognize that it always works out better in the end.*

# Frankie and Leo's Police Station Tour

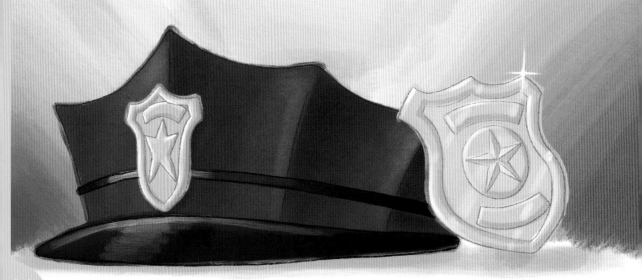

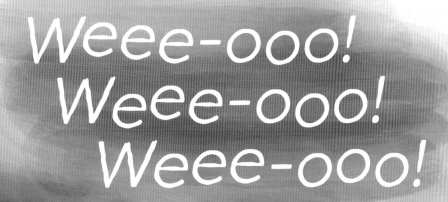

Weee-ooo!
Weee-ooo!
Weee-ooo!

Frankie and Leo's dad
was showing them the sirens
on his police car. Today, their dad was
giving them a tour of the new police station.

After showing them his police car,
their dad recorded their fingerprints.

He took them to an empty
cell where people who are
arrested would stay.

43

He even introduced them
to two police dogs named
BOLO and CODIS.

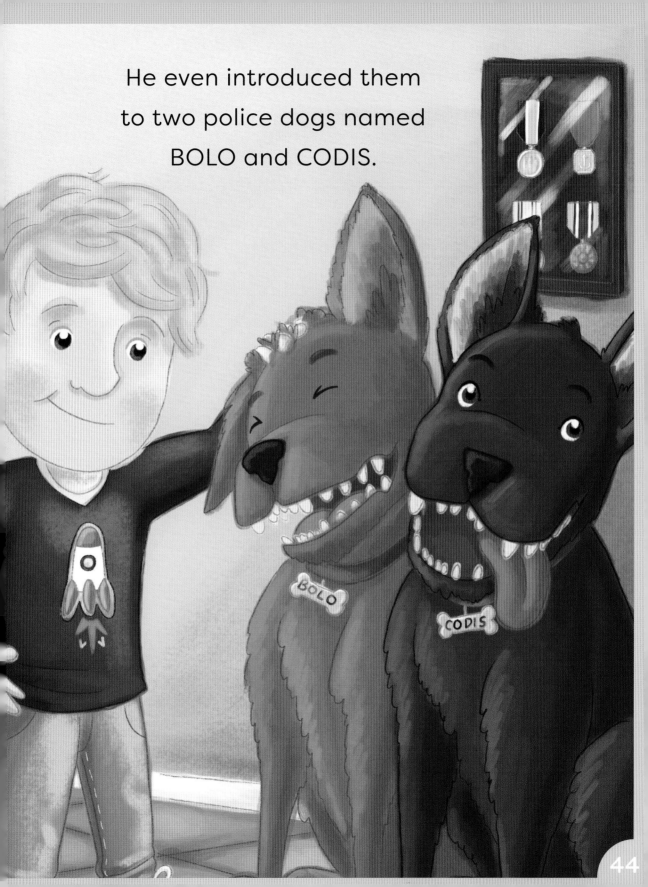

"Boys, wait over here. I need to talk to my partner for just a minute. I'll be right back."

"This has been the best day ever!" Frankie said to Leo.

"Let's play cops and robbers while we wait!" Leo pretended to be a police officer chasing Frankie.

Leo lost control of his walker and banged into a filing cabinet. Everything went **crashing to the floor.**

Frankie quickly helped Leo get up and made sure he wasn't hurt.

48

"Boys, *what happened?*"

Frankie and Leo looked at each other. Leo decided to speak up. "Well, Dad, I..."

Frankie *quickly* interrupted.

"We were waiting here for you. Then a police dog came and knocked Leo into the cabinet."

Their dad looked at them and then glanced around the office.

He knelt down and said,
"Boys, you know as a police officer it is my duty to protect the **truth.** I am trained to know when someone is *lying.* I'm going to give you one more chance to tell me the truth."

"It was my fault, but it was an accident.
Frankie only said that to protect me,"
Leo admitted.

"Thank you, Leo, for being honest.
You both know I would
**rather hear the** truth over a lie.
No matter what happens, always tell the truth."
Frankie and Leo nodded their heads.

"Do you want to see where we keep people who try to hide the truth?"
"Yeah!" Frankie and Leo answered.

Their dad led them to an empty cell. He pretended to lock them up and throw away the key.

"Now, it's time to meet Police Captain Roy."
Their dad led them to the captain's office. The
police captain presented them with their very
own deputy badges. He told them that it should
remind them to always protect the truth.

Frankie and Leo proudly wore
their new badges all the way home.

# THINK & TALK ABOUT IT

## Frankie and Leo's Police Station Tour

*Discuss the story...*

1. What did Frankie and Leo's dad show them at the police station?

2. Should Frankie and Leo have been running around the police station when their dad told them to wait?

3. What happened because they were running around the office?

4. Why did Frankie lie?

5. What does their dad always want them to do?

*Discuss how to apply the story...*

1. Even though Frankie was trying to protect Leo from getting in trouble, do you think Frankie should have lied?

2. Have you ever lied to protect someone?

3. How can telling the truth, even if someone gets in trouble, still be caring?

4. Do you think your parents or guardians would rather hear the truth or a lie?

5. Part of a police officer's job is to protect people. Why do you think it is important to tell them the truth?

FOR PARENTS & MENTORS: *When children have the courage to tell the truth even when they know they've done something wrong, be sure to praise their honesty. Show them the value of honesty by being a good example of what it means to be honest. Also, take the time to point out role models (personally connected or famous) who valued honesty and told the truth. One of the most commended traits of responsible leaders is honesty.*

*Teaching kids to respect the law and authority figures is important. Authority figures are responsible to help keep the community safe. This requires the help and cooperation of people within the community. A child's perception of authority often mirrors their parents' view, so be sure to set a good example in how you talk about them. Explain to your child that obeying and telling the truth helps keep the community safe.*

Meet the

**mvp**kids

featured in
# Lock Up Lying™
with their families

LIAM JOHNSON

**DR. DASHA JOHNSON**
"Mom"

**ESME JOHNSON**
Sister

**JULIA ROJAS**

**COACH SANDRO ROJAS**
"Papá"

**VICTOR ROJAS**
Brother

**FRANKIE RUSSO**

**LEO RUSSO**

**SERGEANT LORENZO RUSSO**
"Dad"

# HONESTY TAG

## HOW TO PLAY:

**1.** Assign roles

**Lie Detector**　　　**Runners**　　　**Truth Doctor**

**2.** The person who is "it" is the **"Lie Detector"** and he or she chases after the **Runners**.

**3.** The **Runners** run around yelling out silly false statements like, "I brush my teeth with mashed potatoes!"

**4.** When the **Lie Detector** tags a **Runner**, the **Runner** must go to a designated jail area.

**5.** The only way a **Runner** can get out of jail is by telling the Truth Doctor a truthful statement.

**6.** However, if a **Runner** gets tagged a second time, he or she also becomes a **Lie Detector** as well.

**7.** The game continues until all the **Runners** are caught.

# Grow up with our MVPkids

Our **CELEBRATE™** board books for toddlers and preschoolers focus on social, emotional, educational, and physical needs. Helpful Teaching Tips are included in each book to equip parents to guide their children deeper into the subject of each book.

Our **Celebrate!™** paperback books for Pre-K to Grade 2 focus on social and emotional learning. Helpful Teaching Tips are included in each book to equip mentors and parents. Also available are expertly written, related SEL curriculum and interactive e-book apps.

Our **Mighty Tokens™** paperback series for Pre-K to Grade 3 helps emerging readers experience positive concepts while reading with parents. This book will reinforce positive concepts as you deposit tokens of affirmation into your child, raising your child to someday be a mighty adult.

Our **Help Me Understand™** series for elementary readers shares the stories of our MVP Kids® learning to understand and manage specific emotions. Readers will gain tools to take responsibility for their own emotions and develop healthy relationships.

# help me BECOME

## Early Elementary

### Ages 4-10

**Help your children grow in character by collecting the entire Help Me Become™ series!**

*Our Help Me Become™ series for early elementary readers tells three short stories in each book of our MVP Kids® inspiring character growth. Each story concludes with a discussion guide to help your child process the story and apply the concepts.*

Stomp Out Selfishness

Defeat Disobedience

Lock Up Lying

Away With Wastefulness

Cure Complaining

STAND Up to Bullies

STAND Together Against Bullying

STAND Down Bullies

Phase Out Forgetfulness

Block Bad Sportsmanship

Limit Laziness

Pick Your Promises

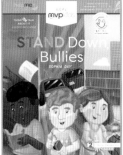
Give Up Greed

Throw Away Theft

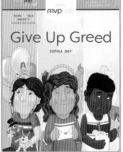

*Learn about our **Social and Emotional Learning Curriculum**, puppets, and more at **www.mvpkidsED.com**.*

*To view our full list of products, visit **www.mvpkids.com**.*

YONG CHEN

LEO RUSSO

FRANKIE RUSSO

JULIA ROJAS

GABBY GONZÁLEZ

ANNIE JAMES

AANYA PATEL

BLAKE JAMES

SARAH COHEN-GOLDSTEIN

LUCAS MILLER

FAITH JORDAN

LeBRON MILLER

EZEKIEL JORDAN

MIRIAM NASSER

OLIVIA WAGNER

LIAM JOHNSON

Get to know our
MVP Kids®!

You will learn and grow
with them from book
to book. Each MVP Kid®
has a personal back story
and unique personality,
making it easier for kids of
all kinds to see themselves
and their friends within
our books!

www.mvpkids.com